Learning Short-take®

SUCCESSFUL PROJECT MANAGEMENT

A step-by-step toolkit for project success

CATHERINE MATTISKE

TPC - The Performance Company Pty Ltd
Level 20, Darling Park
Tower 2, 201 Sussex Street,
Sydney NSW 2000
Australia

ACN 077 455 273
email: tpc@tpc.net.au
Website: www.catherinemattiske.com

© TPC – The Performance Company Pty Limited
First edition published in 2006
Second edition published in 2011
Third edition published in 2022

All rights reserved. Apart from any fair dealing for the purposes of study, research or review, as permitted under Australian copyright law, no part of this publication may be reproduced by any means without the written permission of the copyright owner. Every effort has been made to obtain permission relating to information reproduced in this publication.

The information in this publication is based on the current state of commercial and industry practice, applicable legislation, general law and the general circumstances as at the date of publication. No person shall rely on any of the contents of this publication and the publisher and the author expressly exclude all liability for direct and indirect loss suffered by any person resulting in any way from the use of or reliance on this publication or any part of it. Any options and advice are offered solely in pursuance of the author's and the publisher's intention to provide information, and have not been specifically sought.

For eBook version: By payment of the required fees, you have been granted the non-exclusive, non-transferable right to access and read the text of this e-book on screen. No part of this text may be reproduced, transmitted, downloaded, decompiled, reverse engineered, or stored in or introduced into any information storage retrieval system, in any form or by any means, whether the electronic or mechanical, now known or hereinafter invented, without the express permission of the author.

A catalogue record for this book is available from the National Library of Australia

National Library of Australia
Cataloguing-in-Publication data

Mattiske, Catherine
Successful Project Management: A Step-by-Step Toolkit for Project Success

ISBN 978-1-921547-29-4

1. Occupational training 2. Learning I. Title

370.113

Distributed by TPC - The Performance Company - www.catherinemattiske.com
For further information contact TPC - The Performance Company, Sydney Australia on +61 (02) 9555 1953.

HELLO.

Welcome to the Learning Short-take® process!

This Learning Short-take® is a bite sized learning package that aims to improve your skills and provide you with an opportunity for personal and professional development to achieve success in your role.

This Learning Short-take® combines self study with workplace activities in a unique learning system to keep you motivated and energized. So let's get started!

Step 1:
What's inside?

- Learning Short-take®. This section contains all of the learning content and will guide you through the learning process.
- Learning Activities. You will be prompted to complete these as you read through.
- Learning Journal. This is a summary of your key learnings. Update it when prompted.
- Skill Development Action Plan. Learning is about taking action. This is your action plan where you'll plan how you will implement your learning.

Step 2:
Complete the Learning Short-take®

- Learning Short-takes® are best completed in a quiet environment that is free of distractions.
- Schedule time in your calendar to complete the Learning Short-take® and prioritize this time as an investment in your own professional development.
- Depending on the title, most participants complete the Learning Short-take® from 90 minutes to 2.5 hours.

Step 3:
Meet with your Manager/Coach

- Schedule a 30 minute meeting with your Manager or Coach.
- At this meeting share your completed Activities, Learning Journal and Skill Development Action Plan.
- Most importantly, discuss and agree on how you will implement your learning in your role.

GET VIP ACCESS
TO YOUR MATERIALS

This Learning Short-take® includes an interactive activity book, associated tools and job aids, plus a bonus eBook.

1 Visit
https://www.catherinemattiske.com/books

2 Select your book

3 Click: **VIP ACCESS**

4 Enter the code: SPM2022365

WELCOME

Successful Project Management
A Step-by-Step Toolkit for Project Success

Successful Project Management explores effective strategies to planning and implementing projects within your organization using proven Project Planning tools. You will learn the keys to successful project management by following a structured approach to project planning, implementation and review. By using a real workplace project, **Successful Project Management** strengthens your project management skills. It covers both the essential theory and practical skills for project excellence.

Project Management is a method and set of techniques based on planning, estimating and determining work activities to achieve a desired result on time, within budget and according to specification. During a project's life cycle, project management focuses on three basic parameters: quality, time and cost. A successfully managed project is one that is completed to specified quality, on or before the deadline, and within budget.

Successful Project Management includes the **Problem Summary Report, Project Evaluation Report, Project Plan, Project Status Report, Project Task List**, and the **Work Package Assignment**, provided as free downloadable tools.

1 Learning Short-take® >   Start here

2 Learning Journal   81

3 Skill Development Action Plan   87

4 Quick Reference   93

5 Next Steps   113

"The single best payoff in terms of project success comes from having good project definition early."

RAND CORPORATION

Now let's get started!

"
"Trying to manage a project without project management is like trying to play a football game without a game plan."

K. TATE

Section 1

LEARNING SHORT-TAKE®

WHAT'S IN THIS LEARNING SHORT-TAKE®

"A project is complete when it starts working for you, rather than you working for it."

SCOTT ALLEN

Table of Contents

How to Complete Your Learning Short-take®	5
Activity Checklist	6
Learning Objectives	7
Let's Get Started	8
Part 1: Project Management Fundamentals	11
The Project Management Triangle	13
Essentials for Every Project	16
Part 2: The Project Life Cycle	25
Part 3: Phase 1 - Define the Project	27
Part 4: Phase 2 - Plan the Project	41
Estimating Time and Cost	53
Assess Risk and Contingency Plan	59
Presenting your Project Plan	65
Part 5: Phase 3 - Implement the Project	69
Track and Manage Project With Control Tools	72
Part 6: Phase 4 - Close the Project	77
Inclusion of the Final Project Report	79

HOW TO COMPLETE YOUR LEARNING SHORT-TAKE®

1. **Reflect on your skills and abilities** in project management and how you use this information to improve effectiveness in your role.

2. **Complete the Initial Skills Self-Assessment.**

3. Highlight specific skill areas that you believe you could develop more. Add these to the **Learning Journal**. Add to your Learning Journal as you go.

4. When you have completed this Learning Short-take® **meet with your Manager/Coach**. In this meeting, you will jointly establish a personal **Skill Development Action Plan**.

5. **Subject to your coach's final review** and assessment, you will either sign off the module, or undertake further skill development as appropriate.

"Plans are nothing; planning is everything."

DWIGHT D. EISENHOWER

ACTIVITY CHECKLIST

During this Learning Short-take® you will be prompted to complete the following activities:

- Activity 1 - Initial Skills Self-Assessment — 9
- Activity 2 - Project Essentials — 21
- Activity 3 - Terms & Definitions Match — 23
- Activity 4 - Brainstorm Project Tasks — 50
- Activity 5 - Estimating Time — 55
- Activity 6 - Plan Project Communication & Reporting — 76
- Learning Journal — 81
- Skill Development Action Plan — 87
- The TPC Project Management Tools:
    - Project Plan
    - Project Task List
    - Work Package Assignment
    - Project Status Report
    - Problem Summary Report
    - Project Evaluation Report

"You can only elevate individual performance by elevating that of the entire system."

W. EDWARDS DEMING

LEARNING OBJECTIVES

After you have completed this Learning Short-take®, you should be able to:

- Build direction and standards when managing projects
- Focus on your current projects, looking for improvement opportunities
- Work through the Project Management Life Cycle
- Use standard forms and tools
- Create a Skill Development Action Plan

"Of all the challenges facing project teams, the greatest involves the people themselves."

KEVIN FORSBERG
VISUALIZING PROJECT MANAGEMENT

LET'S GET STARTED

"It is better to have enough ideas for some of them to be wrong, than to be always right by having no ideas at all."

EDWARD DE BONO

Project Management is a method and set of techniques based on planning, estimating and controlling work activities to achieve a desired result on time, within budget and according to specification. During a project's life cycle, project management focuses on three basic parameters: quality, time and cost. A successfully managed project is one that is completed to specified quality, on or before the deadline, and within budget.

This Learning Short-take® allows you plan and implement a project within your organization using proven Project Planning tools. You will learn the keys to successful project management by following a structured approach to planning, implementation and review. The Learning Short-take® uses your own project to improve your project management skills.

 **Complete Activity # 1**
Initial Skills Self-Assessment

ACTIVITY 1: INITIAL SKILLS SELF-ASSESSMENT

Understanding how to plan, implement, control and evaluate a project is essential for all projects regardless of their size or budget. This assessment covers the key skills in project management.

Rate yourself on each of the techniques.
7 is competent and confident, little need for improvement
4 is average, needs improvement
1 is uncomfortable, major need for improvement

- Note specific areas of improvement related to each skill that you would like to develop. Be sure to include your ***reasons*** for your rating in each skill.
- Start thinking about a personal development plan and identify two or three things you could do to improve your skills in this area and write them in the space provided.

I…	Rating	Reasoning
Can define the term 'project management' and its components to others in my organization.	1 2 3 4 5 6 7	
Have created, or could confidently create a common terminology manual for use on projects that I manage.	1 2 3 4 5 6 7	
Can create and manage an effective project team that works together to achieve the project goals.	1 2 3 4 5 6 7	
Can clearly articulate and communicate the project goal and project objectives and measures.	1 2 3 4 5 6 7	
Can write success criteria on which the project will be measured.	1 2 3 4 5 6 7	
Can determine preliminary project resources (including people, equipment, office space, etc) based on the broad project goal.	1 2 3 4 5 6 7	
Can identify project assumptions and risks based on the broad project goal.	1 2 3 4 5 6 7	

ACTIVITY 1: CONTINUED

I...	Rating	Reasoning
Can identify, organize, sequence and communicate project tasks.	1 2 3 4 5 6 7	
Can create a Network Diagram, including a critical path and milestones for a project.	1 2 3 4 5 6 7	
Can estimate project time using weighted averages.	1 2 3 4 5 6 7	
Can estimate project activity cost.	1 2 3 4 5 6 7	
Can assess risks and create appropriate contingencies.	1 2 3 4 5 6 7	
Can implement the project by assigning work packages and can confidently track and control project status.	1 2 3 4 5 6 7	
Can close, document and create a final report for a project including communication to the project team and external suppliers.	1 2 3 4 5 6 7	

Personal development plan ideas:

1

2

Now update your Learning Journal (page 81)

PROJECT MANAGEMENT FUNDAMENTALS

PART 1

PROJECT MANAGEMENT FUNDAMENTALS

What is Project Management?

Project management is a method and a set of techniques for planning, estimating, and controlling work activities to reach a desired result on time, within budget and according to specification.

Planning

Planning involves the establishment of clear and precise objectives (and the work activities that will have to take place to accomplish them) in order to reach a final, stated goal. The goal may involve the solution of a problem, or the achievement of some state or condition different from the present one.

Organizing

In addition to organizing people, project management includes the assembly of the necessary resources, (people, materials and money) for carrying out the work defined in the plan. It also involves creation of the structure needed to execute the plan.

Controlling

Once the resources are assembled into a cohesive structure, it will be necessary to monitor and maintain that structure as the project progresses. Control also includes the creation of a regular reporting structure at identified points through the project life cycle. These reports are designed not only as historical records but also as early warnings of situations and occurrences that are outside expected performance measures.

Change

Where identified situations require change, the project manager will have to institute that change. Project management includes mechanisms for invoking change as necessary.

THE PROJECT MANAGEMENT TRIANGLE

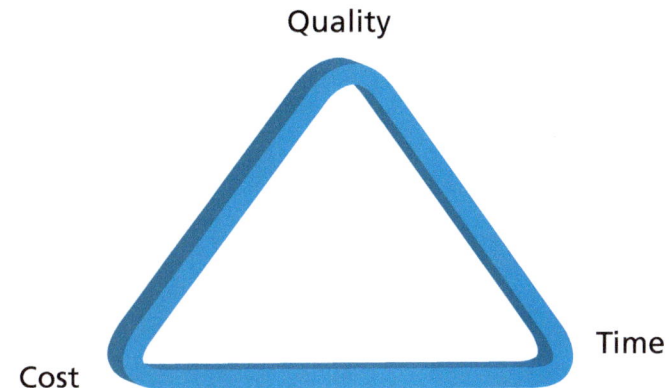

Quality

There are many definitions of quality but quality does not just mean 'luxury' or 'up-market' - these are subjective descriptions. The definitions of quality for the purpose of project management may be defined as:

- Fit for purpose
- Zero defects
- Conforms to specification

To measure the outcomes of the project, project specifications must be set and agreed at the beginning. The success of the project in quality terms will depend upon it meeting those specifications.

> *"Time waits for no one and nowhere is that more true than when managing a project"*
>
> JIM MACINTRYRE
> PROJECT MANAGER AND
> PROJECT MANAGER TEACHER

Cost

This is the project cost and is usually the final cost. The budget is the figure you set out with; that is, what you have available to spend or what you want to spend on the project. But the real cost is what you actually spend when the project is complete.

Time

This is the actual time taken to complete the project. When planning a project you can start with a required end date and work back to the present, allocating enough resources to complete the project on time.

Alternatively, you can plan all your tasks, allocate the required time against available resources and produce a given end date.

In reality, most projects are a compromise of these two approaches and during the progress of the project there will be fluctuations in timing even if the end date remains the same.

Creating Balance

The project management triangle works best when all three elements are in balance and no one element is considered more important than the others. In reality however, this is rarely the case. Even where a project starts with the elements in balance, this is likely to change during the life of the project.

Changes may be caused by factors beyond the control of the project team or they may be as a result of team actions, but changes are not necessarily problems.

It is up to the customer and project manager to agree the initial targets for quality, cost and time.

The questions to be asked are:

- If quality is the priority, do we need more resources? That is, can we put in more cost, or do we lengthen the project?
- If cost is the priority, can we reschedule or change our objectives?
- If time is the priority, can we add more resources? That is, increase cost or alter our objectives?

"An event or situation for which there is no corrective action that can be taken and which can endanger part or the entire project."

DAVID NICKSON
& SUZY SIDDONS

ESSENTIALS FOR EVERY PROJECT

Common Vocabulary

Common project management vocabulary is essential given that:
- Most companies don't have a common language for projects
- Words are used differently across projects, companies and industries
- Terminology manuals when they exist are often imprecise
- Individual interpretation causes on-going miscommunication

A terminology manual

A terminology manual, tailored to the project at hand, can go a long way to fixing these problems, and should be appropriate to the industry, company and the specific project.

Project Managers should hold their teams accountable to the project vocabulary. It is reasonable to have team members certify that they have read the project terminology manual and that they are committed to using it.

Teamwork

Team effectiveness relies on many things: chemistry, attitudes and motivational sources. Achieving real teamwork depends on:
- Forming a group capable of becoming a team
- Creating and sustaining a team environment, and
- Inspiring team growth through leadership

The fundamentals of an effective team environment

Effective teams share several common characteristics. They can articulate a common goal that they are committed to achieve. They acknowledge their interdependency and mutual respect.

They have accepted a common set of boundaries on their actions - a common code of conduct for the performance of the task. They have accepted the fact that there is one reward they will all share. They share a team spirit and a sense of enjoyment when working together.

Our dilemma today is that merely having a project manager and a kick-off event is insufficient to sustain real teamwork.

"Project management is like juggling three balls - time, cost and quality."

G. REISS

Five fundamentals of effective teamwork

1 - Common goals

Building teamwork begins with clearly defining the group objectives and outlining the various roles and responsibilities required to achieve the objectives. Gaining consensus on the top-level goal is often easy. You must probe to the second or third tier to reveal and resolve real conflicts around goal expectations.

2 - Acknowledged interdependency and mutual respect

In his book *"7 Habits of Highly Effective People"*, Stephen Covey says, "The cause of almost all relationship difficulties is rooted in conflicting or ambiguous expectations around roles and goals."

At the beginning, one very revealing team effort is defining roles. After team orientation and goal setting, the task of preparing personal job descriptions provides an important way of getting feedback and confirmation regarding team role perceptions. This step is the vehicle for the team to acknowledge interdependency and to establish expectations.

- Define the specific functions, tasks and individual responsibilities
- Develop an organizational structure and define team interdependencies
- Define the scope of authority of each member

3 - A common code of conduct

Common codes of conduct are usually well documented by company or government policies. However, these may not be well known to all team members, and gray areas involving contractor and customer interfaces may not be understood or interpreted consistently. The project manager is responsible for reviewing these issues, together with the relevant company policies, to ensure that all team members are sensitized to potential problems.

To be effective, a common code of conduct needs to:

- Establish rules of behavior
- Reach consensus on the definition of an ethical code of conduct
- Document the most significant factors

4 - Shared rewards

Effective team rewards begin with fair and equitable compensation for each position on the team. Shared rewards may also be by way of team recognition.

"A project without a critical path is like a ship without a rudder."

D. MEYER,
ILLINOIS CONSTRUCTION LAW

5 - Team spirit and energy

This quality depends on personal attitudes as well as company culture and begins with:

- An agreement to pool resources
- Interdependence rather than independence
- Desire to do whatever is necessary to succeed
- Placing team needs above one's own needs.

"Individual commitment to a group effort - that is what makes a team work a company work, a society work, a civilization work."

VINCE LOMBARDI

Complete Activity # 2
Project Essentials

Complete Activity # 3
Terms & Definitions Match

ACTIVITY 2: PROJECT ESSENTIALS

For your chosen project answer the following questions:

1. In general, what are the 'quality' expectations for your project that have either been clearly stated or implied by your organization?

___

2. In general, how would you balance quality, time and cost for your project?

___

3. Do you have a common terminology manual for your project? If not, then what will be your process to develop one?

___

ACTIVITY 2: CONTINUED

4. Reflect on the five fundamentals of teamwork. Complete the table below - what can you specifically do to promote and encourage teamwork within your project team?

Project Manager Specific Activities		
At Project Start		
For the Project Duration	Daily	
	Weekly	
	Monthly	
On Achievement of Project Milestones		
At Project End		

Now update your Learning Journal (page 81)

ACTIVITY 3: TERMS & DEFINITION MATCH

Draw a line to match the project management term with it's correct definition.

Project Teams	This involves the establishment of clear and precise objectives (and the work activities that will have to take place to accomplish them) in order to reach a final, stated goal.
Planning	Includes the assembly of the necessary resources, (people, materials and money) for carrying out the work defined in the plan.
Project Quality	Monitor and maintain the project and also create a reporting structure at specified points through the project life cycle.
Controlling	A method and a set of techniques based on the accepted principles of management used for planning, estimating, and controlling work activities to reach a desired end result on time, within budget and according to specification.
Project Cost	▪ Fit for purpose ▪ Zero defects ▪ Conform to specification
Project Management	The budget is the figure you set out with; that is, what you have available to spend or what you want to spend on the project. But the real cost is what you actually spend when the project is complete.
Organizing	In project management terms this is the actual time taken to complete the project.
Project Time	A list of commonly used terms and acronyms used for a specific project.
Common Terminology Manual	▪ Can articulate their common goal that they are committed to achieve. ▪ Acknowledge their interdependency coupled with mutual respect. ▪ Have accepted a common set of boundaries on their actions - a common code of conduct for the performance of the task. ▪ Have accepted the fact that there is one reward they will all share. ▪ Have a spirit and a sense of enjoyment when working together.

Activity # 3 - Check Your Answers

Planning	This involves the establishment of clear and precise objectives (and the work activities that will have to take place to accomplish them) in order to reach a final, stated goal.
Organizing	Includes the assembly of the necessary resources, (people, materials and money) for carrying out the work defined in the plan
Controlling	Monitor and maintain the project and also create a reporting structure at specified points through the project life cycle.
Project Management	A method and a set of techniques based on the accepted principles of management used for planning, estimating, and controlling work activities to reach a desired end result on time, within budget and according to specification.
Project Quality	• Fit for purpose • Zero defects • Conform to specification
Project Cost	The budget is the figure you set out with; that is, what you have available to spend or what you want to spend on the project. But the real cost is what you actually spend when the project is complete.
Project Time	In project management terms this is the actual time taken to complete the project.
Common Terminology Manual	A list of commonly used terms and acronyms used for a specific project.
Project Teams	• Can articulate their common goal that they are committed to achieve. • Acknowledge their interdependency coupled with mutual respect. • Have accepted a common set of boundaries on their actions – a common code of conduct for the performance of the task. • Have accepted the fact that there is one reward they will all share. • Have a spirit and a sense of enjoyment when working together.

Now update your Learning Journal (page 81)

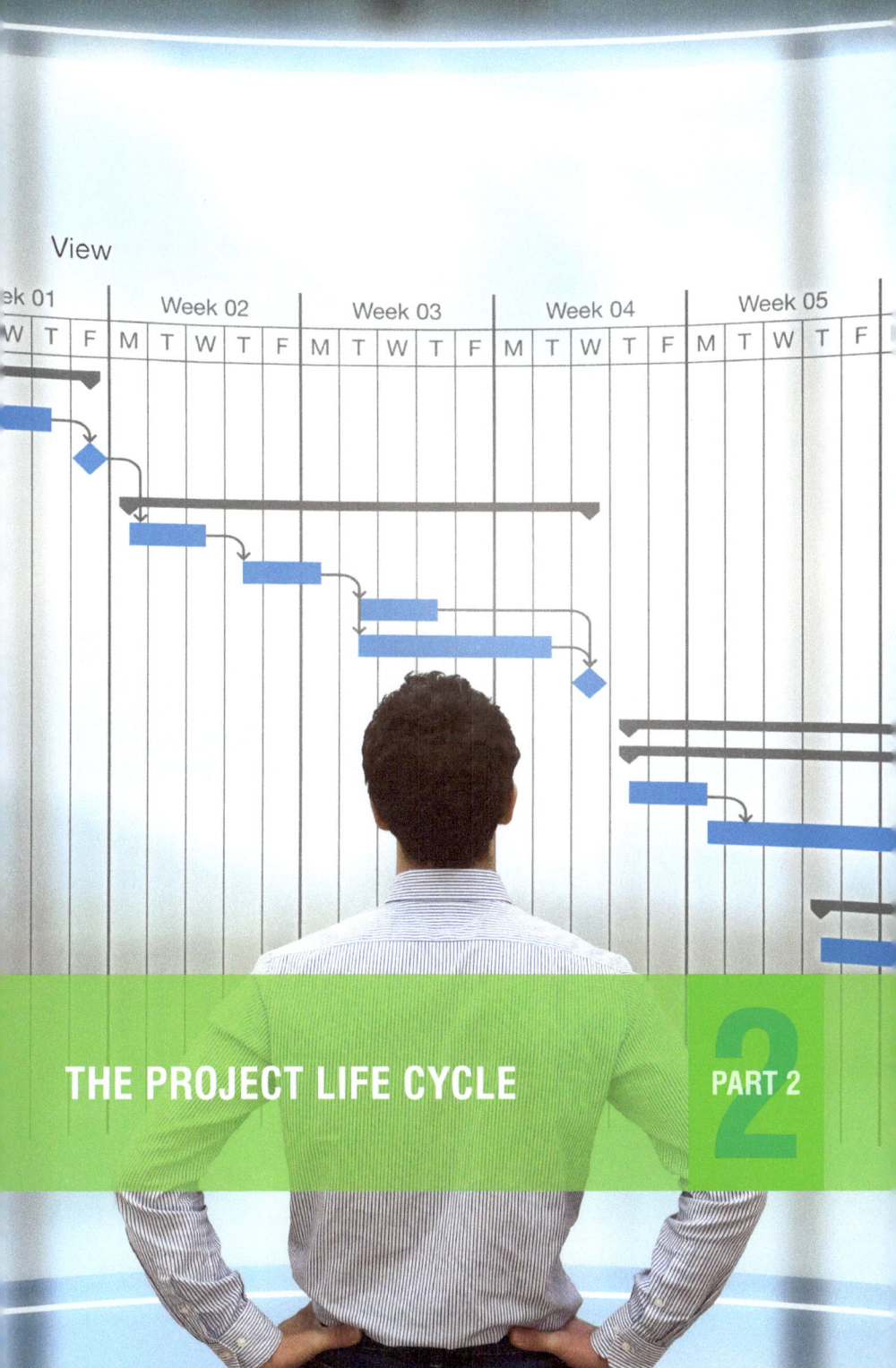

4-Phase Project Life Cycle

1 Define	2 Plan	3 Implement	4 Close
State the Problem / Opportunity	List Specific Deliverables	Assign Work Packages	Formally Close the Project
Write Project Goal	Identify Milestones	Track Projects	Final Project Report
Customer Focus	List Project Tasks	Plan Project Communication & Reporting	
List Project Objectives	List Project Exclusions	Manage Project Change	
Evaluate Project Success Criteria	List Project Deliverables	Contain Risk - Project Reviews & Meetings	
Determine Preliminary Resources	Estimate Time and Cost		
Schedule Project	Assess Risk & Contingency Plan		
Identify Assumptions & Risks	Indicate Resource Requirements		
List Related Projects	Obtain Stakeholder Sign-off		
Obtain Preliminary Approval			

PHASE 1 - DEFINE THE PROJECT

PART 3

PHASE 1 - DEFINE THE PROJECT

1
Define
State the Problem / Opportunity
Write Project Goal
Customer Focus
List Project Objectives
Evaluate Project Success Criteria
Determine Preliminary Resources
Schedule Project
Identify Assumptions & Risks
List Related Projects
Obtain Preliminary Approval

The focus of this phase is to produce a Project Overview. It serves as:

- General information for other managers. Keeping others informed is a routine activity in successful project management
- An early statement of the goal and direction of the project; and
- A statement of the problems and opportunities to be addressed by the project.

Once the project is approved for a go-ahead, the project overview becomes the foundation for the more detailed planning activities that follow next. It will serve as a reference base whenever questions or conflicts arise as to the future direction of the project. During the early stages of implementation it will be a tool for recruiting and training the project team.

Finally, it provides a control point for reporting project progress and an audit point for evaluating the effectiveness of the project in achieving stated goals and objectives.

Step 1 - State the Problem/Opportunity

The need arises from a problem or situation (internal or external) that either threatens the organization or presents it with a valued opportunity. This part of the project overview documents not only the need but also the benefit to the organization for undertaking the project.

The statement should be short, crisp, and to the point. It clearly outlines what is expected, by whom and with what resources.

Step 2 - Write Project Goal

Every project has one major goal to be accomplished and several objectives, which support the goal. The goal is the global statement of purpose and direction toward which all objectives work activities and tasks will point.

The project goal statement

The project goal statement is important for two reasons:
- It is a clear statement of what is to be done
- It is an event whose completion can be measured

The project goal directs the course of the effort. The goal will be the standard for resolving conflicts, for clarifying expectations, for requesting and justifying resources. The goal is the most important statement initiating the project.

Examples of action-oriented goal statements

- Connect James Road and Swan Street via a tunnel running under the Madison River and open it to traffic by December 31.

- Design a software package that performs basic financial analysis for small to medium fashion businesses and complete pilot testing by September.

- Obtain a MBA from Benzyls College within 3 years.

- Create a new Performance Review program and launch it globally on February 15, with the first round of Performance Reviews completed by all managers by May 31.

Note that each of these goal statements tells precisely what will be done and by when. The end point may have to be revised after further review, but at this point the end date shows finality to the project.

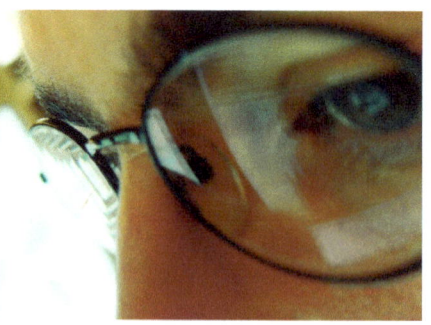

Step 3 - Customer Focus

Whether the end user of the project is a department or business unit in the organization or the purchaser of the organization's products or services, the trend in successful organizations is to have them involved in the project. Identify customers and list their expectations in relation to communication and project deliverables.

Step 4 - List the Project Objectives

Objectives represent major components of the project. The term milestone often replaces the term objectives. Objectives are not the actual work that is accomplished but subgoals that direct work activity. They are more precise statements than the goal statement and, like goal statements, are action-oriented.

By specifying objectives we begin to view the project in terms of its major components. Objectives are a crude roadmap that helps decision-makers and other members of the management team to understand the scope of the project. They also provide a basis for determining resource requirements and setting the project timeline.

"Without goals, and plans to reach them, you are like a ship that has set sail with no destination."

FITZHUGH DODSON

During this Learning Short-take®, you are encouraged to work on a real-life project. Please choose a project now that you will use in selected Learning Short-take® Activities. It is advised that you choose a straight forward project that you are yet to plan. You will use the Learning Short-take® planning tools to create your plan.

Download the TPC Project Plan from https://www.catherinematttiske.com/books

THE PERFORMANCE COMPANY PROJECT PLAN

For your project planning you will use The Performance Company Project Plan. Download it now.

ACTIVITY USING TOOL

TPC Project Plan - Define Your Project
Start the First Section

Using your own real-life project, complete **only** the following sections of the TPC Project Plan

- Project Plan: Planning and Approval Document (Cover Sheet):
  - Project Name
  - Position
  - Date Created
  - Date Last Updated
  - Document Author Name
  - Division
  - Version Number
  - Online Information

- Project Plan: Phase 1 - Define Project
  - Project Name/Project Manager
  - Problem/Opportunity
  - Project Goal
  - Customer Focus
  - Project Objectives

You will create the remaining parts of the TPC Project Plan later.

Now update your Learning Journal (page 81)

Define the Project (continued)

Step 5 - Evaluate Project Success Criteria

The following examples include criteria for measuring success:

- At least 245 of the 280 delegates will register and attend the annual conference.

- The new product introduction will generate sales of $350,000 in the first six months.

- The new order entry system will be considered successful if the average time from order entry to order fulfilment is less than five working days; the average order value exceeds $1,000; less than 2% of orders are backordered; there is less than one customer complaint per $100,000 ordered.

At this early stage of project preparation, it may be beneficial to be in contact with those individuals and groups who will be involved in the project in order to gather a preliminary list of success criteria against which the project outcomes can be measured. This criteria will most likely be revised as the project plan progresses.

Step 6 - Determine Preliminary Resources

Resources not only include money, but also human resources, materials, and financial capital. Included on your list of resources will be:

- People (how many, who, when, and for how long)
- Equipment (what pieces, when and for how long)
- Office space, or online workspace and systems if your project team is virtual (Appropriate space for the project managers, assistant project manager, team members and other support staff, as required)

Two scenarios in considering preliminary resources

There are two scenarios to consider:

- The resources were determined without Project Manager input
- The Project Manager determines the needed resources based on the project plan

First scenario - without Project Manager input

When the Project Manager is appointed he or she will need to review what has already been allocated prior to their start on the project and ensure that the allocated resources are realistic.

Based on existing contracts and agreements with customers, the Project Manager may have little choice, regardless of the adequacy of the resources given to the project. Once the formal planning process is completed, the Project Manager will require documentation to argue for the necessary resources to complete each work assignment.

Second scenario - with Project Manager input

The Project Manager may be asked to present a preliminary plan in which they 'guesstimate' required resources. This scenario is clearly preferable to being told what has been allocated by another person who may or may not be skilled or fully informed on the project requirements.

Step 7 - Schedule Project

Identify the likely project start and delivery/end dates for the project.

Take into account time taken for the Project Plan to be created and the Project Proposal to be approved by Stakeholders. The likely delivery/end date should be based on initial knowledge and research, and may be amended during or after the completing the Project Proposal.

Step 8 - Identify Assumptions and Risks

The project often needs to be 'sold' to key stakeholders. Therefore, the project overview must be a persuasive statement. In order to effectively sell an idea, product or service, the Project Manager must carefully consider what's at stake.

"Judge others by their questions rather than by their answers."

VOLTAIRE

Questions to ask as a guide to stating assumptions and risks

Using the list of project objectives ask the following questions:

- What resources are required to complete this objective? What risks are associated with obtaining any of these resources in a timely manner?

- What problems and delays are likely to occur in completing this objective?

- What effect(s) will delays have on the budget and overall project schedule and plan?

- What are the probable time, money and personnel cost overruns to complete this project?

- What assumptions can be made to realistically correct for delays in completing this objective within given resources and constraints?

Step 9 - Related Projects and Activities

Often there are related projects either internal or external to the project. List these and state the relationship to this project.

Step 10 - List Stakeholders

Key Stakeholders are people or business areas which influence the project. Key stakeholders are often internal and external to the organization and may be required to approve the project at all stages of the Project Life Cycle.

Key Stakeholders may be listed as 'participating', (i.e. they are actively involved in the project) or 'affected' (i.e. that they are impacted by the project outcome or project development). In addition, list the impact the key stakeholder has on the project (e.g. decision maker) or the project has on them (e.g. significant impact).

Throughout the project, the Project Manager sets the level and type of communication required for Key Stakeholders.

"Risk management can only work if the whole project team is committed to it in theory and in practice."

DAVID NICKSON
& SUZY SIDDONS

 Use the downloaded **TPC Project Plan** from https://www.catherinematttiske.com/books

THE PERFORMANCE COMPANY PROJECT PLAN

Continue using The Performance Company Project Plan.

ACTIVITY USING TOOL

TPC Project Plan - Define Your Project Complete the First Section

Using your real-life project, continue to complete the TPC Project Plan for the following:

- Project Plan: Phase 1 - Define Project
    - Success Criteria
    - Preliminary Resources
    - Initial Scheduling Information
    - Assumptions
    - Risks
    - Related Projects and Activities
    - Stakeholder Information

- Phase 1 Approval - Obtain Preliminary Approval (Complete details ready for signature)
    1 - Preliminary Approval Checklist
    2 - Preliminary Approval Details (List Project Manager's Name)
    3 - Preliminary Approval by Key Stakeholders (List Names/Department)

Now update your Learning Journal (page 81)

 Use the downloaded **TPC Project Plan** from https://www.catherinematttiske.com/books

THE PERFORMANCE COMPANY PROJECT PLAN

Continue using The Performance Company Project Plan.

SEEK PRELIMINARY APPROVAL

Using your real-life project, continue to complete the TPC Project Plan.

Obtain preliminary approval for your project, and complete signatures in your Project Plan.

- Phase 1 Approval - Obtain Preliminary Approval (Complete signatures)
  - 2 - Preliminary Approval Project Manager's Signature and date
  - 3 - Preliminary Approval by Key Stakeholders Signature/s and date

Now update your Learning Journal (page 81)

> *"When planning for a year, plant corn. When planning for a decade, plant trees. When planning for life, train and educate people."*
>
> CHINESE PROVERB

PHASE 2 - PLAN THE PROJECT

PART 4

PHASE 2 - PLAN THE PROJECT

2
Plan
List Specific Deliverables
Identify Milestones
List Project Tasks
List Project Exclusions
List Project Deliverables
Estimate Time and Cost
Assess Risk & Contingency Plan
Indicate Resource Requirements
Obtain Stakeholder Sign-off

Step 1 - List Specific Deliverables

Specify Work Packages - Using Project Task List

The Project Task List is the document that organizes and summarizes the tasks necessary to complete the project. The Project Task List assists the Project Manager to:

- Identify the major tasks in the project and ensure that all the work that needs to be done is clearly indicated.
- Organize tasks in the most logical sequence so the tasks can be efficiently scheduled.
- Identify tasks that need to be assigned to various team members.
- Identify the resources necessary to complete each task so a budget can be developed.
- Communicate the work to be done in an unambiguous way so team members understand their assigned jobs and responsibilities for completing the project.
- Organize related tasks into logical milestones.

Step 2 - Identify Milestones

Using Network Diagram & Milestones

Example of Basic Network Diagram

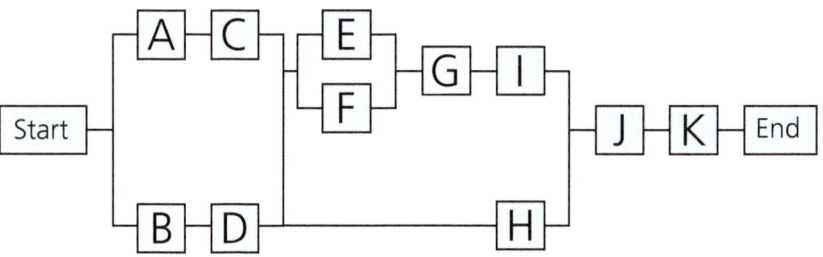

A properly sequenced network diagram will:

- Show the sequence of tasks in completing a project.
- Identify milestones in the project that can be used for monitoring progress and accomplishments.
- Show the interrelationships of tasks in different parts of the project tasks.
- Establish a vehicle for scheduling tasks.

"Don't be afraid to give your best to what seemingly are small jobs. Every time you conquer one it makes you that much stronger. If you do the little jobs well, the big ones will tend to take care of themselves."

DALE CARNEGIE

Precedence Relationships in a Project Network

Precedence defines task sequencing order and how tasks are related to one another in the plan.

Though some tasks must precede others, many tasks can be started in parallel with other tasks. This leads to the other important diagramming, the concept of simultaneous activities.

The concepts of precedence and simultaneous work are important because the relationships between tasks ultimately will establish the basis for scheduling a project. The goal in developing the network diagram is to identify activities that can occur in parallel and to specify the precedences that exist among the activities.

Symbols and Conventions

Creating a Network Diagram is a process of linking tasks. Tasks are shown in boxes and connected by lines.

Diagramming relationships: Basic conventions

The following lists some of the basic conventions (rules) in putting tasks down in a network diagram:

- **Placing tasks in horizontal order** from left to right in the network represents the defined sequences of tasks.

- **Tasks that can happen at the same time** are shown in columns. These are called "parallel tasks" because the work can happen in parallel with other work on different rows.

- **Drawing lines** from tasks to task, indicating that the task on the left must be completed before the task on the right can begin and shows the precedences between tasks and milestones. The task that must be completed first is called the precedent task. The task that starts after the precedent task is called the dependent task. That's why the network diagram is said to reveal the dependencies among tasks.

- **Lines among tasks** can cross the rows to show how tasks in the various sequences relate to each other.

- One task may depend on the completion of multiple tasks or milestones. The precedences for all of these tasks must be shown by drawing lines from the **precedent tasks to the dependent task**. A task may start independently of some tasks but still be dependent on others. Lines are only drawn between tasks with dependency.

- A task without a precedent task or milestone can logically be started at any time after the initial "start project" task because it has no other dependent relationships. Put such a task in its own row.

"A milestone is a fixed point taken at any given time during the progress of a project where actual progress can be compared directly against estimated progress."

JEAN HARRIS
SHARPEN YOUR TEAM'S SKILLS
IN PROJECT MANAGEMENT

Five steps to create a Network Diagram

Most network diagrams start with a box labelled "Start Project" and an end with a box labelled "Project Finished".

1 - List the Tasks using the Project Task list

For a network diagram each task should have a unique identifying number or other code. A network diagram will lay out the work units or individual tasks.

2 - Establish the Interrelationships between the tasks

- What tasks must precede this task? That is, what other tasks must be completed before this one can be started?
- What tasks follow this task? Or, what tasks cannot be started until this task is complete?
- What tasks can take place concurrently with this one? Or more simply, what tasks can be worked on at the same time this one is being completed?

3 - Identify Milestones you want to specify

Milestones are not tasks. Milestones do not take effort; they are just convenient markers for summarizing work that has been performed to that point on the network diagram.

4 - Layout the tasks and milestones as a network

5 - Review the logic of the network

- Are the tasks properly sequenced?
- Are all the precedences identified?
- Is there some precedence that isn't really required?
- Are all of the tasks really necessary?
- Does the completion of the tasks in the network represent the accomplishment of everything necessary to meet the project goals that have been specified?

"The Critical Path is a sequence of project activities for which there is minimum or zero slack. The Critical Path can be shown in bold."

KEVIN FORSBERG, VISUALIZING PROJECT, MANAGEMENT

The critical path

The expected project duration time determined from the critical path analysis and the contracted project completion date provide useful pieces of information for making management decisions. For example:

- The scheduled start and completion date for each activity.
- The activities whose completion must occur exactly as scheduled in order for the project to be kept on schedule.
- The amount of delay that can be tolerated in non-critical path activities without causing a delay in the scheduled project completion date.
- Activities whose resources might be diverted to critical path activities if the need arises.

Example of **Critical Path**

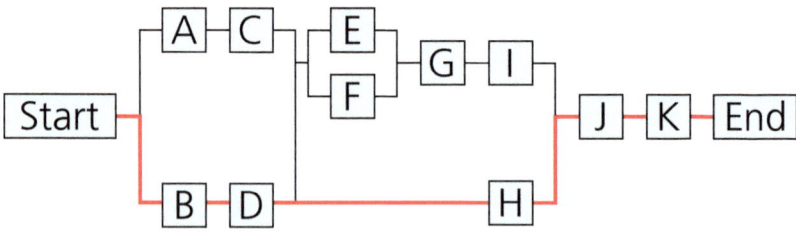

 Use the downloaded **TPC Project Plan** from https://www.catherinematttiske.com/books

THE PERFORMANCE COMPANY PROJECT PLAN

Continue using The Performance Company Project Plan.

ACTIVITY USING TOOL

TPC Project Plan - Plan Your Project Start the Next Section

Continue to complete the TPC Project Plan for the following:

- Project Plan: Phase 2 - Plan Project
  - What are the specific deliverables of the project?
  - Identify Milestones

You will complete more of this section later.

Now update your Learning Journal (page 81)

 **Complete Activity # 4**
Brainstorm Project Tasks

ACTIVITY 4: BRAINSTORM PROJECT TASKS

Next, brainstorm and identify your project tasks. **Do this now for your real-life project.**

Depending on the size of your project you may elect to brainstorm project tasks alone or with a small group of key people (e.g. you would likely invite a project team member, key stakeholder, customer, subject matter expert and other key people to be a part of this group).

To help you, review the 'Rules of Brainstorming' on the next page.

If you elect to brainstorm alone, use the space below to record your ideas.

ACTIVITY 4: CONTINUED

Rules of Brainstorming - 'How To'

You will need a large whiteboard or flipchart paper on which to write, and a large felt-tipped marker. If your project team is virtual, most virtual meeting software includes a digital whiteboard feature. Or use an online collaboration and whiteboarding app such as Canva Whiteboards, Google Jamboard or MIRO.

- The question or issue is written up for all to see.
- Appoint a scribe. The scribe must write down every idea as quickly as possible without censoring or qualifying (abbreviation is allowed). The scribe may also act as the group motivator, constantly calling for new ideas. Alternatively, another person may take the mediator role. The scribe should work in front of the group. All ideas written up must be visible to the whole group.
- Operate with a group of 7-10 people. 15 people is generally the upper workable limit. Try to obtain a mix of people from different backgrounds, divisions, departments and disciplines.
- Have the group define the task in clear terms. Avoid self-limiting definitions. For example, instead of asking "How can we eliminate overtime?", ask "How can we improve use of employee work hours?". The latter question is more open and will give you more options.
- Ask for crazy ideas early in the brainstorm session. This will stimulate freewheeling ideas which go beyond the established wisdom and known solutions.
- An irrevocable rule of brainstorming is that there should be no criticism or evaluation of ideas at this stage. If someone disagrees with an idea, or doesn't think it feasible, they should not say so, but should offer an alternative idea (without explanation).
- Seek a large number of ideas. Their quality is irrelevant. Evaluation comes later.
- Link different ideas together. Expand on ideas. Play with them. Encourage the group to be lively - it is a catalyst of creativity.
- Keep the pace fast. Keep comments to a minimum. The scribe should stimulate the group: for example "That's great! Is there any other way we could do it?", "What else could we do?", "How else could it be done?"
- Be aware of the group energy. If the group has run out of ideas, move on to evaluation.

To discover more on brainstorming, ideas generation and other creativity techniques for individuals and groups, refer to Learning Short-take®: 'Creative Business Thinking'

Now update your Learning Journal (page 81)

 Download the **TPC Project Task List** from https://www.catherinematttiske.com/books

THE PERFORMANCE COMPANY PROJECT TASK LIST

First use The Performance Company Project Task List. Download it now.

Then you will continue to use The Performance Company Project Plan - keep it on hand.

ACTIVITY USING TOOL
TPC Project Task List - List Project Tasks

Using the results of Activity 4 - Brainstorm Project Tasks, organize your brainstormed tasks into logical groups. Then sequence the tasks into logical order. **Use The Performance Company Project Task List to record your tasks.**

CONTINUE USING TPC TOOL
Continue Phase 2 - Plan Your Project

Using the TPC Project Plan, complete the following:

- Project Plan: Phase 2 - Plan Project
  - Identify Project Tasks: List the major task groups and ensure that you refer to an attached Project Task List.
  - Project Exclusions
  - Project Dependencies

You will complete the rest of this section later.

Now update your Learning Journal (page 81)

ESTIMATING TIME AND COST

The time to complete an activity is varied. That is, if a given activity were done over and over again one would expect the completion times to vary somewhat.

Reasons for this variation include:

- Skill levels of the people doing the activity
- Machine variations
- Material availability
- Unexpected events (sickness, natural disasters, employee strikes, industrial accidents, employee turnover, etc.)

We know these events happen, but we cannot predict their occurrence on a specific project or activity with any accuracy. In some way, however, we are compelled to account for them.

Estimating Time - 3 variants

There is a statistical relationship that accounts for these variations quite well and is very easy to use. It requires only that we obtain three estimates of activity completion time:

O **Optimistic completion time:**
The time that will be required if everything goes perfectly.

P **Pessimistic completion time:**
The time that will be required that if everything that can go wrong does go wrong (Murphy's Law) but the activity is still completed.

M **Most likely completion time:**
Time required under more normal situations.

Weighted Average Formula

Average activity completion time = E
Optimistic time = O
Pessimistic time = P
Most likely time = M

The following formula gives that weighted average:

$$E = (O + 4M + P) / 6$$

Estimating Time Example

Production time to manufacture Red Japanese-style lanterns.

O	Optimistic time	3 Hours
P	Pessimistic time	5.5 Hours
M	Most likely time	3.5 Hours

E = (O+4M+P)/6
E = (3+(4X3.5)+5.5)/6
E = (3+14+5.5)/6
E = 22.5/6
E = **3.75**

Complete Activity # 5
Estimating Time

ACTIVITY 5: ESTIMATING TIME

Review Components of Time

E	Average activity completion time
O	Optimistic time
P	Pessimistic time
M	Most likely time

Weighted Average Formula

The following formula gives the weighted average:

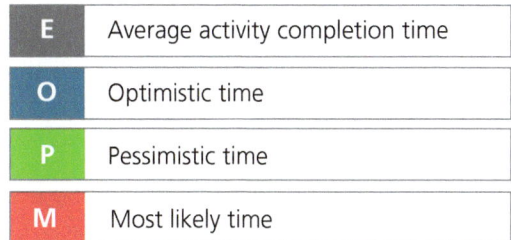

$$E = (O + 4M + P) / 6$$

Activity - Calculate the Time Estimate

Using the weighted average formula, calculate the time estimate for the following Project Task.

O	Optimistic time	2 days
P	Pessimistic time	10 days
M	Most likely time	5 days

Your Answer: _____

Activity # 5 - Check Your Answer

O	Optimistic time	2 days
P	Pessimistic time	10 days
M	Most likely time	5 days

$E = (O + 4M + P)/6$

You should have calculated using the following formula:

$E = (2 + (4 \times 5) + 10)/6$

Answer: **5.33 days**

Now update your Learning Journal (page 81)

Estimating Activity Cost

In order to ensure accurate estimates, estimating costs is often a two-step process. These steps lead to a more accurate cost estimate by incorporating the knowledge gained during the design phase of the project combined with knowledge from previous projects.

- **Step 1 - Initial Estimates:** The Initial Rough Estimate is developed during the Initiating Phase and is based on the information provided in the first part of the Project Plan together with information from previous projects the project manager has managed. This estimate will be presented in the project plan in Part 1, Preliminary Resources (see TPC Project Plan).

- **Step 2 - Final Estimates:** After initial approval and during the Planning Phase, the project requirements will be developed for key stakeholders and customers to review and approve. These will further clarify and define the project costs. The project manager will usually provide a complete and detailed cost estimate of the project effort. This estimate will be presented in the project plan in Part 2, Estimate Time and Cost (see TPC Project Plan) and will usually be supported with attached cost schedules.

Four Cost Categories

There are typically four major cost categories that may be defined for any activity:

1 Labor

2 Materials

3 Other direct (travel, telephone, contracted services etc)

4 Indirect (overhead) - In some cases indirect costs may be a fixed percentage of total direct costs attributable at the project level rather than at the activity level.

 Use the downloaded **TPC Project Plan** from https://www.catherinematttiske.com/books

THE PERFORMANCE COMPANY PROJECT PLAN

Continue using The Performance Company Project Plan.

ACTIVITY USING TOOL

Continue Phase 2 - Plan Your Project

Continue to complete the TPC Project Plan:

- Project Plan: Phase 2 - Plan Project
  - Estimate Time & Cost (for each Project Task)

Now update your Learning Journal (page 81)

ASSESS RISK AND CONTINGENCY PLAN

By identifying potential risks to a project you put the project team in the position of someone who is 'forewarned and therefore forearmed'. By being aware of what the risks are you will be able to identify warning signs and act quickly to minimize or eliminate their impact.

In addition, by identifying the high risk areas to a project it is possible to make a decision early on, that a project is too risky to continue and therefore avoid the situation of starting a project that is doomed to failure.

The benefits are the increased chance of delivering the project on time and to budget, combined with significantly decreased chance of being ambushed by the unexpected.

"The goal of the risk and constraint analysis is to establish the feasibility of the project within the constraints of economy, politics, laws, and organizational structure that limit your business. This risk and constraint analysis establishes whether the goals of the project you just defined are really feasible."

SUNNY & KIM BAKER

The Difference between Constraints and Risks

Constraints, unlike risks, are known in advance. If you have only $10,000 to buy a car, that's a constraint. No matter how much you want that new luxury vehicle, $10,000 won't buy it for you. Constraints are the real world limits on the possibilities for your projects. Violate the constraints in defining your project, and the project will fail in some way. The job of the project manager is to make sure you understand the constraints of your project and work within their limits.

Sources of Risk

There are many sources of risk to a project, however they generally fall into two categories.

- **External risks:** risks affecting the viability of the project that come from the outside world and business environment.
- **Internal risks:** risks that come from within the project, eg. The tools used by the project team, technical issues, staff ability, etc.

Identifying Risks - Small vs. Large Projects

Which risk identification approach is more appropriate?

For small projects the brainstorming approach is the superior one because duplicate risks are identified more quickly and the meeting provides an opportunity to present risk management in a positive light and to raise the general understanding of the risks to the project as a whole.

For larger projects this approach is more difficult to achieve for logistical reasons; it may be too expensive and/or impractical to get all those needed together in a manageable forum. Here, it is better to adopt the structured interview method and accept that it will take a little longer to perform the risk analysis.

In both cases it is also necessary to **assess the importance of the risks**. As this will be taking place during the start-up stages of the project the information that people have available to them will be either speculative or based on experience.

Risk Assessment & Taking Action

There are many ways of assessing risks to a project. A simple one is to define all risks in terms of two factors:

- **Probability** - percentage (to nearest 10% or high, medium and low), plus
- **Impact on project** - high, medium and low:
  - High - significant impact, schedule and costs severely affected
  - Medium - less serious, impact on only part of the project
  - Low - negligible effect

Risk Decision Matrix

Identified risks are plotted onto a matrix according to their probability and impact.

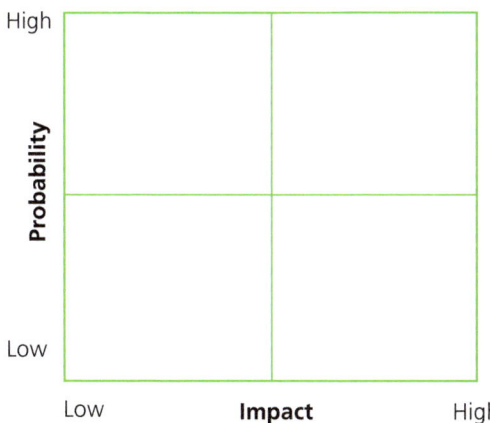

 Use the downloaded **TPC Project Plan** from https://www.catherinematttiske.com/books

THE PERFORMANCE COMPANY PROJECT PLAN

Continue using The Performance Company Project Plan.

ACTIVITY USING TOOL
Continue Phase 2 - Plan Your Project

Continue to complete the TPC Project Plan for the following sections:

- Project Plan: Phase 2 - Plan Project
  - Risk Assessment & Contingency Planning
  - Other Information (as necessary for your project)
- Schedule A - Indication of Resource Requirements
  - Indication of Systems
  - Indication of Human Resources
  - Indication of Post Implementation Support

Now update your Learning Journal (page 81)

Seek Customer/Stakeholder sign-off

The Reality Check before Sign-off

Before submitting the plan for final approval, you need to perform one last cross-check of your planning efforts. The following steps for cross-checking a project plan are:

- From the **network diagram**, match the tasks, durations, and dates to the scheduling worksheet. Also, match the resources to the scheduling worksheet. Finally, match the task to the activities shown in the Project Task List.

- **Verify the numbers** on the budgeting worksheet and re-total them to ensure they match your existing estimate.

- Study the tasks on the **critical path**. Is the right path selected? Are there any tasks that require more time? Have you separated the labour required from the duration on each task?

- **Verify that the milestones** (if you chose any) make sense as a means of summarizing the main activities in a project.

- Check that the start date and finish date are still reasonable. Also, verify that you have accounted for all holidays and vacations in the schedule.

 **If you didn't assemble either a Network Diagram or a written Project Plan it's almost impossible to cross-check a project. A plan is an absolute requirement of success in project management.**

> "A primary cause of lateness and overspending in projects is the failure to allow for contingencies and to assess risks before the project starts and to identify new ones as the project progresses."
>
> DAVID NICKSON & SUZY SIDDONS

Verify Resource Availability

With all tasks and amounts verified, it's time to verify resource availability one last time before the plan goes to management or customers for approval. You might have had to modify your plan due to errors or a delayed start date.

Check the revised plan that all resources will be available in the right timeframe. If the planning and approval cycle has been lengthy, people, vendors, and equipment might no longer be ready when you need them: people might have been reassigned or in the worst case scenario, vendors might have gone out of business.

Should a vital resource become unavailable, you will have to find a suitable replacement, modify the project (if possible) to accommodate actual availability, or change the project's scope so you don't need the missing resource.

PRESENTING YOUR PROJECT PLAN

Before presenting, study the presentation of the plan from an outsider's viewpoint. Do the tasks explain themselves or is additional notation required? Are the tasks equal in scope (or almost)? Is the presentation clear and organized? Is the level of presentation appropriate for the scope of the project?

You must be prepared to justify your choices, dates, and budgets. You'll need a compelling reason why each task is required, and present well thought-out risks and contingencies together with the associated budget justification.

Always start with an overview of the plan and then move on to details. The goal of the presentation is to present the overall structure and objectives of the project, answer questions, and establish your credibility as the project planner (and Project Manager).

Too much detail in the presentation can be as devastating as too little. With too much detail in your presentation, you'll be bombarded with questions and arguments from management about the details. Avoid this by using milestone summaries of the tasks so managers don't fail to see the big picture during your presentation. Keep the meeting short (one-hour) and focused.

The result of your presentation will either be the approval (by signature) of the project (which is unlikely on a first presentation of a large project) or a request to make revisions. If real objections crop up, stop the presentation and reschedule the meeting after the plan has been modified.

 Use the downloaded **TPC Project Plan** from https://www.catherinematttiske.com/books

THE PERFORMANCE COMPANY PROJECT PLAN

Continue using The Performance Company Project Plan.

ACTIVITY USING TOOL
Continue Phase 2 - Plan Your Project

Complete the TPC Project Plan for the following:

- Phase 2 Approval - Stakeholder Sign-off
    - 1 - Complete Approval Checklist
    - 2 - Complete Approval Details, including Project Owner and Project Manager signatures

Now update your Learning Journal (page 81)

 Use the downloaded **TPC Project Plan** from https://www.catherinematttiske.com/books

THE PERFORMANCE COMPANY PROJECT PLAN

Continue using The Performance Company Project Plan.

SEEK STAKEHOLDER SIGN-OFF

Using your real-life project, complete the TPC Project Plan. Obtain Stakeholder Sign-off

- Phase 2 Approval - Stakeholder Sign-off
  - 3 - Sign-off by Key Stakeholders
  - 4 - Sign-off by Financial Executive
  - 5 - Sign-off by Cost Centre Owners

Complete final page of the Project Plan

- Project Plan Change History / Attachments
  - List Attachments, e.g. Project Task List

Now update your Learning Journal (page 81)

If you are able to obtain Preliminary Approval by Key Stakeholders for your real-life project, do so now. With the approval complete you will continue to use your real-life project when completing the remaining activities.

If you are not in a position to gain Preliminary Approval or are waiting for Preliminary Approval by Key Stakeholders continue with this Learning Short-take®. Each Activity will provide you with appropriate instructions.

"Plans are only good intentions unless they immediately degenerate into hard work. "

PETER DRUCKER

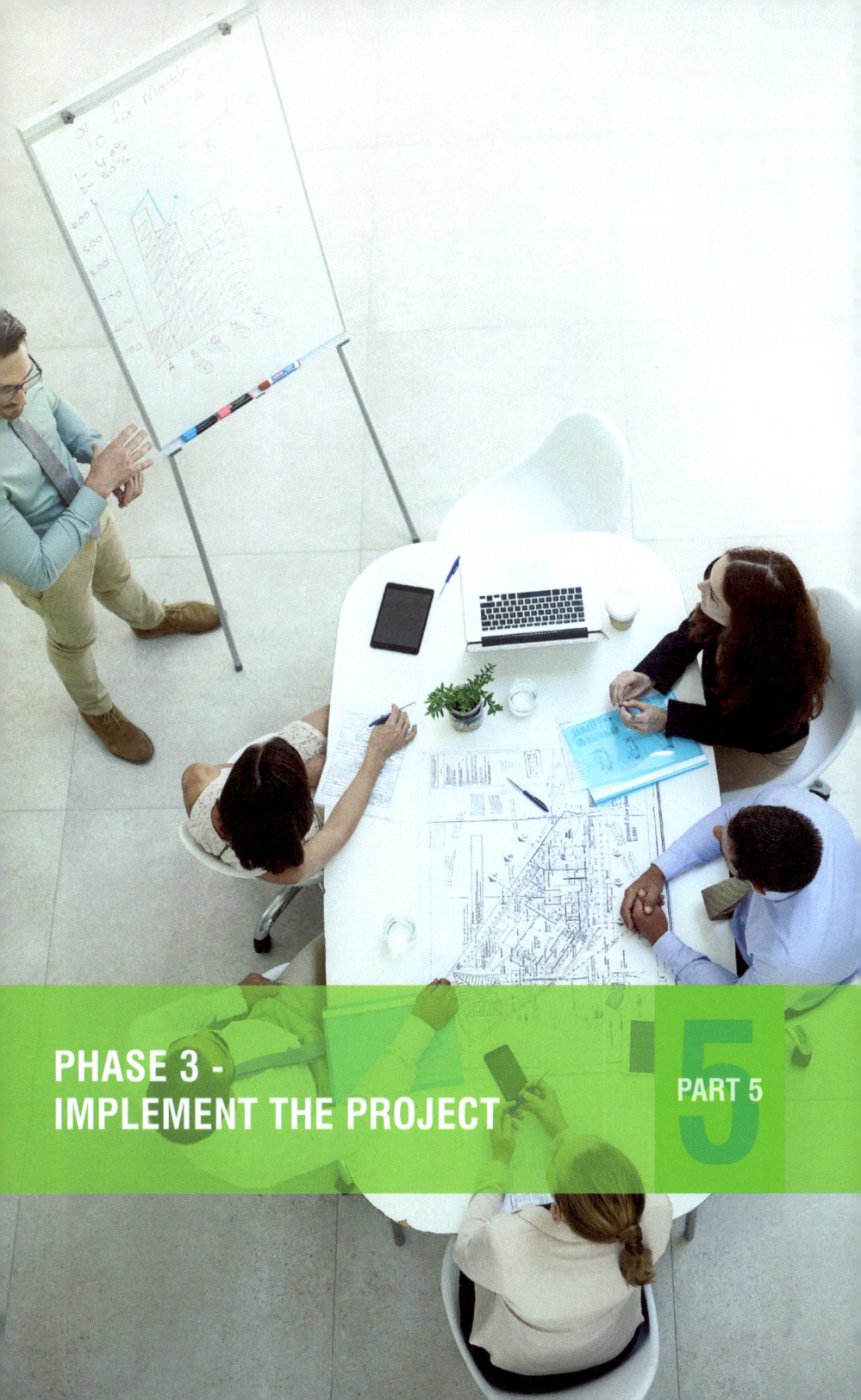

PHASE 3 - IMPLEMENT THE PROJECT

PART 5

PHASE 3 - IMPLEMENT PROJECT

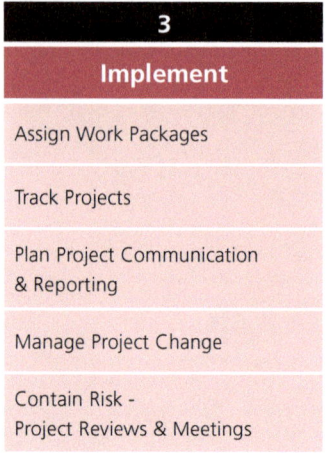

Assign Work Packages

Work packages refer to the basic unit of work that takes place in the project. A work package consists of one continuous activity. The work package is assigned to one person who has the authority and access to resources needed to complete the assignment. It will have definite beginning and end tasks so that its completion will be easily measured and clearly observed. Using work packages includes the following benefits:

- To inform all parties working on the activity, as well as all predecessor and successor activities, of the contracted deliverables and expected end dates.
- To record the project and be of value not only to the project manager but also to future project managers.
- To provide sufficient detail and description of all the tasks that comprise the work package and of the relationship of the work package to other work packages and to the project.
- To be presented in a format that can be updated and provide information for periodic project status reports.
- To hold the work package manager responsible for the successful completion of the tasks that comprise the work package.
- To serve as a reference point for clarifying issues and conflicts that may arise.

 Download the Work Package Assignment tool from https://www.catherinematttiske.com/books

THE PERFORMANCE COMPANY WORK PACKAGE ASSIGNMENT

You will use The Performance Company Work Package Assignment. Download it now.

ACTIVITY USING TOOL

Assign Work Packages

- Review and complete the **Work Package Assignment**
- If necessary, modify or amend the tool for your project needs

Now update your Learning Journal (page 81)

TRACK AND MANAGE PROJECT WITH CONTROL TOOLS

Controls are designed to focus on one or more of the three major components of a project - performance levels, cost and time schedules. Three reasons for using controls are:

To track progress	The Project Manager will want to have in place a periodic (at least monthly) reporting system that identifies the status of every activity in the project. These reports should summarize progress for the current period as well as for the entire project.
To detect variance from plan	In larger projects (say, 50 or more activities) reports that say everything is on schedule and on budget are too long (and usually too boring) to be read and synthesized. Exception reports, variance reports and graphical reports provide information for management decision making and provide it in a concise format.
To take corrective action	Once a significant variance from the plan occurs, the next step is to determine whether corrective action is needed and then act appropriately. In complex projects this will require examining a number of "what ifs". When problems occur in the project, delays result and the project falls behind schedule. For the project to get back on schedule, resources will have to be reallocated.

Prepare Status Reports

Variance reports provide a snapshot in time (the current period) of the status of the project or any of its activities. It does not report how the project or activity reached that status. Variance reports may be used to report project variances or activity variances.

For each report period the total resources used (by activity or task within activity) are computed. Comparing these figures against the planned use of resources (planned-actual) provides the project manager with one measure of project status.

Positive variance	Positive variances may allow for replanning that will bring the project in ahead of schedule, under budget, or both. If the project manager has multiple project management responsibilities, there may be opportunities to reallocate some resources from projects with positive variances to projects with negative variances.
Negative variance	This condition may arise for reasons beyond the control of the project manager or project team. Regardless of the reason, the project manager must find ways to correct the situation. The objective will be to bring the project back into agreement with the plan.

Getting Back on Schedule

In its simplest form getting back on schedule involves reallocating resources from non-critical path activities to critical path activities. Slack management is a term often used for this task.

Download the Project Status Report from
https://www.catherinematttiske.com/books

THE PERFORMANCE COMPANY PROJECT STATUS REPORT

You will use The Performance Company Project Status Report. Download it now.

ACTIVITY USING REPORTS
Project Status Report

- Review carefully the following the TPC Project Status Report
- If necessary, modify or amend the Report for your project needs
- Complete the report as appropriate during your project

Now update your Learning Journal (page 81)

 Download the Problem Summary Report from https://www.catherinematttiske.com/books

THE PERFORMANCE COMPANY PROBLEM SUMMARY REPORT

You will use The Performance Company Problem Summary Report. Download it now.

ACTIVITY USING REPORTS
Problem Summary Report

- Review carefully the TPC Problem Summary Report
- If necessary, modify or amend the Report for your project needs
- Complete the report as appropriate during your project

Now update your Learning Journal (page 81)

Complete Activity # 6
Plan Project Communication & Reporting

ACTIVITY 6: PLAN PROJECT COMMUNICATION & REPORTING

Using The Performance Company Reports as a guide, plan the communication strategy for your project.

Sample:

Group Name/ Individual Name	Project Communication (for duration of project)	Frequency	Tool/Form/ Method
Key Stakeholders (as per Project Plan)	Project Status Report	Weekly	TPC Project Status Report
Management Team	Top 10 Problem Summary Report	Weekly	TPC Problem Summary Report
Key Stakeholders	Budget Update	Monthly	Project Budget

Your Project:

Group Name/ Individual Name	Project Communication (for duration of project)	Frequency	Tool/Form/ Method

Now update your Learning Journal (page 81)

PHASE 4 - CLOSE THE PROJECT

PART 6

PHASE 4 - CLOSE

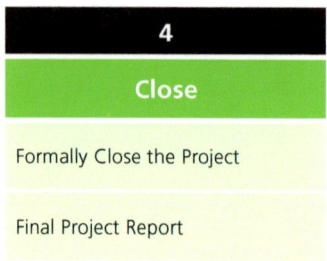

Formally Close the Project

Final Project Report

"A judgement has to be made where to draw the line between useful work and diminishing returns."

DAVID NICKSON
& SUZY SIDDONS

Closing a project includes some or all of the following activities:

- To formally close outside contractual relationships with suppliers, manufacturers, customers, and other budgeted parties who expect an earlier, agreed-upon termination of services.

- To formally terminate project team member assignments.

- To obtain client acceptance of the project work and deliverables.

- To ensure that all deliverables have been installed or implemented according to time, budget and specification.

- To ensure that adequate project documentation and baseline information are in place to facilitate interactions or changes that may need to occur in the future.

- To issue and obtain sign-off on the final report or status of the project, which shows that the contracted deliverables have been satisfactorily implemented.

- To terminate all external and internal relationships.

- Create a Final Project Report.

INCLUSION OF THE FINAL PROJECT REPORT

The following elements are usually included:

- Overall success and performance of the project (using the post-implementation audit results).
- Organization and administration of the project.
- Techniques used to accomplish project results.
- Assessment of project strengths and weaknesses.
- Recommendations from the project manager and team for continuation or closure of the project.

Benefit of the TPC Project Evaluation Report

This report is designed as a discussion guide during the final project team meeting. The project team would discuss each question and note the answers. After the meeting, the Project Manager would compile the answers and submit it as the 'Analysis, Reflection & Key Learnings' part of the Final Project Report to key stakeholders. See above for other inclusions within the Final Project Report.

"Give us the tools and we'll do the job."

WINSTON CHURCHILL

 Download the Project Evaluation Report from https://www.catherinematttiske.com/books

THE PERFORMANCE COMPANY PROJECT EVALUATION REPORT

You will use The Performance Company Project Evaluation Report. Download it now.

ACTIVITY USING REPORTS
Project Evaluation Report

- Review carefully the TPC Project Evaluation Report
- Modify or Amend the Report for your project needs
- At the end of your project, complete this report

Now update your Learning Journal (page 81)

Section 2
LEARNING JOURNAL

The Learning Journal is used throughout the process to record your key learnings, hot tips and things to remember.

Update your Learning Journal at anytime. Ensure you complete your Learning Journal after you finish each activity. Then turn back to the Learning Short-take® to continue your learning.

LEARNING JOURNAL

As you work through this Learning Short-take®, make detailed notes on this page of the lessons you have learned and any useful skill areas. For each lesson or refresher point think about how you could further develop this skill. Your coach will want to discuss these with you in your Skill Development Action Planning meeting.

*"…that is what learning is.
You suddenly understand something you've understood all your life, but in a new way."*
DORIS LESSING

"Act as though it were impossible to fail."
WINSTON CHURCHILL

> *"The wise do at once what the fool does later."*
> BALTASAR GRACIAN (1601-58), SPANISH JESUIT PRIEST AND AUTHOR.

Learning or Idea	Action to be taken	Result Expected

Learning Journal - continued

Learning or Idea	Action to be taken	Result Expected

> *"Anyone who stops learning is old, whether at twenty or eighty."*
> HENRY FORD

Learning or Idea	Action to be taken	Result Expected

"Of all the things I've done, the most vital is coordinating the talents of those who work for us and pointing them towards a certain goal."

WALT DISNEY

Section 3

SKILL DEVELOPMENT ACTION PLAN

Your Skill Development Action Plan is the last Step in the process. After you have completed the Learning Short-take® and all Activities, update your Learning Journal, then complete this section.

SKILL DEVELOPMENT ACTION PLAN

This is the most important part of the program - your individual Skill Development Action Plan.

You need to complete this plan before meeting with your manager or prior to on-going coaching. You will discuss it in detail with your manager or coach as he or she will ensure that you have everything you need to complete the tasks and activities.

Once you have completed your **Skill Development Action Plan** schedule a meeting time with your manager or coach to review your plan. Take your Learning Short-take® and all other documentation received during the training course to this meeting.

Remember - you have committed to your **Skill Development Action Plan**, and need to make time to complete your tasks!

"The mind, once stretched by a new idea, never regains its original dimensions."
OLIVER WENDELL HOLMES

"Whatever you can do or dream you can - begin it. Boldness has genius, power and magic."
JOHANN WOLFGANG VON GOETHE

"Imagination is the eye of the soul."
JOSEPH JOUBERT (1754-1824)

Task or activity (Be specific)	Measure (this will help you to know you have achieved it)	Date (Be specific)
Reflect on your Learning Journal. Transfer action items that you can apply to your job. Ensure that you include some 'stretch goals' and also a blend of short, medium and long term goals.	Apart from you, who else is needed to assist you in achieving your goal.	Be specific. A general date such as 'Quarter 1', 'August', or 'by end of year' is vague and more likely to result in not achieving your target. Be specific – e.g. 22nd November.

IDEAS FOR DISCUSSION WITH MY MANAGER

Ideas

CONGRATULATIONS!

You've now completed this Learning Short-take®.

Meet with your Manager/Coach to discuss your Skill Development Action Plan.

Suggested Reading

Chang, Richard Y & Kelly, P. Keith, "Step-by-Step Problem Solving, Richard Chang & Associates Inc, USA, 1993

Covey, Stephen R, "The Seven Habits of Highly Effective People", Information Australia, Simon & Schuster, New York, 1989

Forsberg, K. "Visualizing Project Management", John Wiley & Sons, 1996

Higgins, James M, "101 Creative Problem Solving Techniques, New Management Publishing Company, Inc, 1994

Lewis, James P, "Fundamentals of Project Management", American Management Association, 1997

Nickson, David & Siddons, Suzy, "Managing Projects", Made Simple Publishing, 1997

Nutting, John & White, Gillian, "The business of communicating", McGraw Hill Book Company, Sydney, 1993

QUICK REFERENCE

This Quick Reference provides you with a summary of key concepts, models and reference material from Learning Short-takes®. We have also included some quotations to ponder.

Use this section as a quick reference to keep your learning active.

Quick Reference

Glossary of Terms

Action Plan - A plan that describes what needs to be done and when it needs to be completed. Project plans are action plans.

Activity - A specific project task that requires resources and time to complete.

Contingency plan - An alternative for action if things don't go as planned or if an expected result fails to materialize.

Control - A process for assuring that reality or actual performance meets expectations or plans. Control often involves the process of keeping actions within limits by making adjustments to a plan to assure that certain outcomes will happen.

Cost-benefit analysis - An analysis, often stated as a ratio, used to evaluate a proposed course of action.

Critical path - The sequence of tasks that determine the minimum schedule for a project. If one task on the critical path is delayed, the schedule will be late.

Customer - Any individual, group or organization that receives a product or service from you, or that pays or arranges with you for the product or service to be provided.

Delight - To exceed customer's unstated needs

Glossary of Terms

Deliverables - The clearly defined results, goods or services produced during the project or at its outcome. Deliverables and goals are often synonymous. Deliverables, like may include organizational attributes, reports and plans as well as physical products or object.

Duration - The period of time over which a task takes place, in contrast to effort that is the amount of labor hours a task requires. Duration establishes the schedule for a project. Effort establishes the labor costs. Each task in a project has a duration, usually specified in workdays or portions of work days, that may or may not be different than the amount of effort (or labor) required to complete the task.

Functional Management - The standard departments of a business organization that represent individual disciplines such as engineering, marketing, purchasing and accounting.

Gantt Chart - A chart that uses timelines and other symbols to illustrate multiple, time-based activities or projects on a horizontal time scale.

Key Customer - A customer whose satisfaction is one of your top priorities based on how they fit in with your organization's strategy and how much they depend on your organization to achieve success.

Quick Reference

Glossary of Terms

Milestone (1) - A clearly identifiable point in a project that summarizes the completion of a related or important set of tasks. Milestones are commonly used to summarize the important events in a project for managers and stakeholders who don't want or need to see the details in a project plan.

Milestone (2) - Summarizes the completion of an important set of tasks of the completion of an important event in a project such as a subproject.

Milestone (3) - A logical combination of tasks or a subproject.

Network diagram - The logical representation of tasks that defines the sequence of work in a project. A network for a simple project might consist of one or two pages. On a large project, several network diagrams might exist: one for the overall project based on the project milestones and one for each subproject that leads to the completion of a milestone.

Partnering - Collaborating with a customer or supplier to listen and respond to a customer's needs.

Precedence - When one task must be completed before another task can be started the first task is said to have precedence over the other.

Glossary of Terms

Project - A project is a sequence of tasks with a beginning and an end that uses time and resources to produce specific results. A project has a specific, desired outcome, a deadline or target date when the project must be done, and a budget that limits the amount of people, supplies, and money that can be used to complete the project.

Project duration - The time it takes to complete the entire project, from starting the first task to finishing the last task.

Project Goal - The specifications of what you hope to achieve at the end of the project.

Project Management - The process of combining systems, techniques and people to complete a project within established goals of time, budget and quality.

Project Manager - Any person who takes overall responsibility for coordinating a project, regardless of size, to make sure the desired end result comes in on time and within budget.

Scope - The size of the project.

Stakeholder - People who have a personal or entrepreneurial interest in the end results of a project. Not all Stakeholders are involved in completing actual work on a project. Common Stakeholders include customers, managers, corporate executives and representatives of government agencies.

Quick Reference

Glossary of Terms

Subtask - A portion of the complete task. For example, the task might be to write the articles for a newsletter, while a subtask might be to write the lead article for the newsletter. See Element of Work.

Supplier - Any individual, group, or organization that you receive a product or service from, or that you pay or arrange with for the product or service to be provided.

Task - A task is a cohesive unit of work on a project - one that's not too big or too small to be tracked. A task may include several steps (or subtasks) that are conceptually related.

Work breakdown structure (1) - A hierarchical chart used to organize the tasks of a project into related areas. It often is completed as a tree diagram or as an outline. In the WBS, milestones and tasks are clearly defined. The completed WBS can be used for budgeting and personnel selection purposes as well as scheduling and network diagramming.

Work breakdown structure (2) - A basic project diagram or listing that documents and describes all the work that must be done to complete the project. The WBS forms the basis for costing, scheduling, network diagramming and work assignments.

Work process - A standard sequence of work activities or procedures through which a product or service is developed, produced, delivered, managed or controlled.

> **Risk management can only work if the whole project team is committed to it in theory and in practice.**
>
> David Nickson & Suzy Siddons

Quick Reference

Project Management Triangle

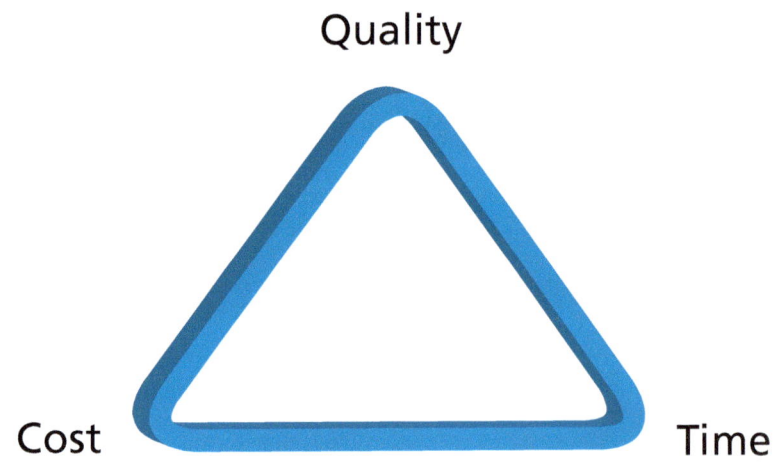

The Project Life Cycle

4-Phase Project Life Cycle

1. Define	2. Plan	3. Implement	4. Close
State the Problem / Opportunity	List Specific Deliverables	Assign Work Packages	Formally Close the Project
Write Project Goal	Identify Milestones	Track Projects	Final Project Report
Customer Focus	List Project Tasks	Plan Project Communication & Reporting	
List Project Objectives	List Project Exclusions	Manage Project Change	
Evaluate Project Success Criteria	List Project Deliverables	Contain Risk - Project Reviews & Meetings	
Determine Preliminary Resources	Estimate Time and Cost		
Schedule Project	Assess Risk & Contingency Plan		
Identify Assumptions & Risks	Indicate Resource Requirements		
List Related Projects	Obtain Stakeholder Sign-off		
Obtain Preliminary Approval			

Quick Reference

Phase 1 - Define the Project

1
Define
Step 1 - State the Problem / Opportunity
Step 2 - Write Project Goal
Step 3 - Customer Focus
Step 4 - List Project Objectives
Step 5 - Evaluate Project Success Criteria
Step 6 - Determine Preliminary Resources
Step 7 - Schedule Project
Step 8 - Identify Assumptions & Risks
Step 9 - List Related Projects
Step 10 - Obtain Preliminary Approval

Phase 2 - Plan the Project

2
Plan
Step 1 - List Specific Deliverables
Step 2 - Identify Milestones
Step 3 - List Project Tasks
Step 4 - List Project Exclusions
Step 5 - List Project Deliverables
Step 6 - Estimate Time and Cost
Step 7 - Assess Risk & Contingency Plan
Step 8 - Indicate Resource Requirements
Step 9 - Obtain Stakeholder Sign-off

Quick Reference

Phase 3 - Implement the Project

3
Implement
Step 1 - Assign Work Packages
Step 2 - Track Projects
Step 3 - Plan Project Communication & Reporting
Step 4 - Manage Project Change
Step 5 - Contain Risk - Project Reviews & Meetings

Phase 4 - Close the Project

4
Close
Step 1 - Formally Close the Project
Step 2 - Final Project Report

Quick Reference

Project Plan

Go to **https://www.catherinemattiske.com/books**
to download this tool

Project Task List

Go to **https://www.catherinemattiske.com/books** to download this tool

Quick Reference

Work Package Assignment

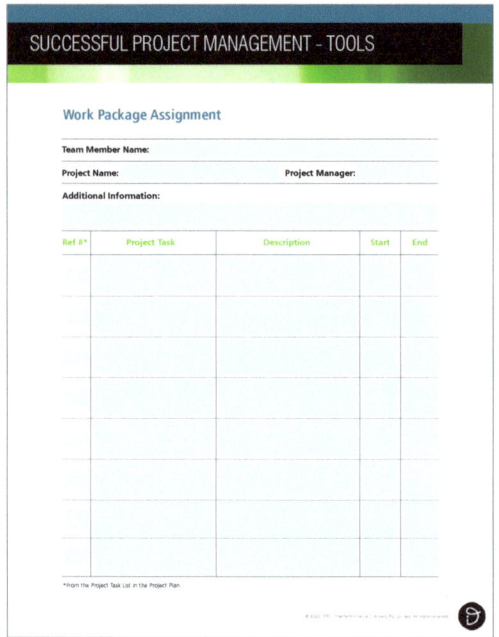

Go to **https://www.catherinemattiske.com/books** to download this tool

Project Status Report

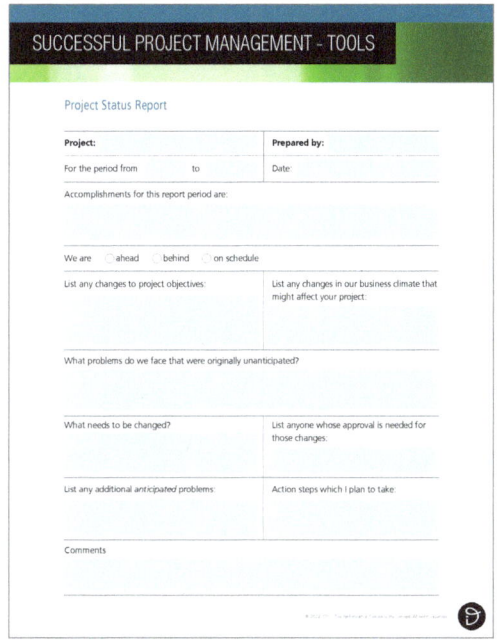

Go to **https://www.catherinemattiske.com/books** to download this tool

Quick Reference

Problem Summary Report

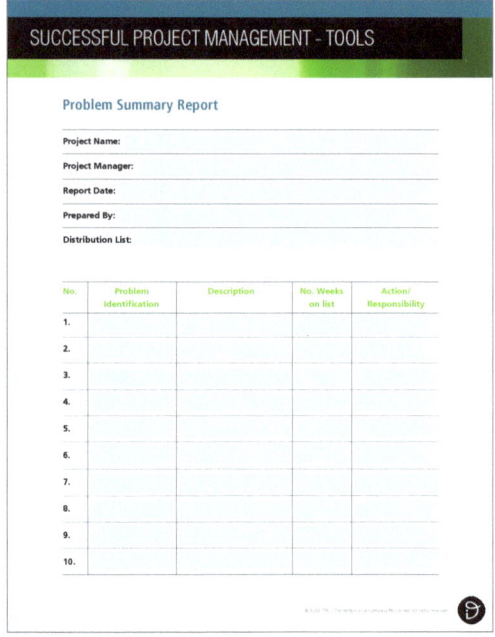

Go to **https://www.catherinemattiske.com/books** to download this tool

Project Evaluation Report

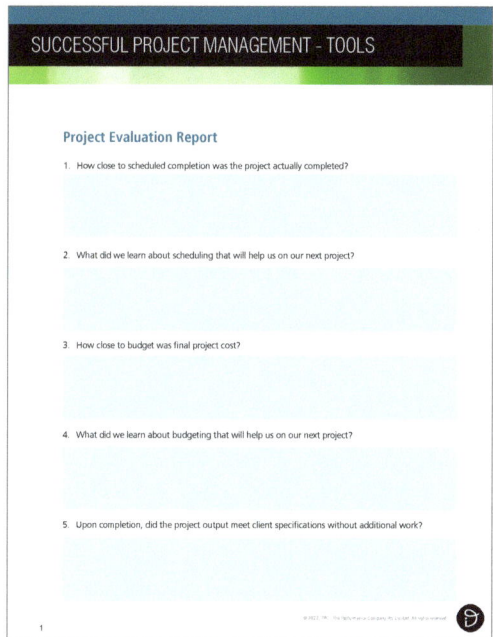

Go to **https://www.catherinemattiske.com/books** to download this tool

Quick Reference

> **A milestone is a fixed point taken at any given time during the progress of a project where actual progress can be compared directly against estimated progress.**
>
> Jean Harris

NEXT STEPS

Congratulations! You have now completed this Learning Short-take® title. The entire list of Learning Short-takes® can be found on the catherinemattiske.com website.

In this section we have suggested Learning Short-take® titles for you that will build your learning. You may order these Learning Short-takes® online at https://www.catherinemattiske.com/books or from your bookstores.

Persuasive Presentation Skills
Create, Prepare and Design with Confidence

Learning Short-take® Outline

Persuasive Presentation Skills combines self-study with realistic workplace activities to provide presenters with the key skills and techniques to prepare and deliver dynamic presentations. After assessing your current approach to preparing and delivering presentations, **Persuasive Presentation Skills** will help you develop unique and innovative strategies to improve your presentation success from small meetings to large audiences. You will learn to effectively plan your communication by using a real-life upcoming presentation.

A dynamic and powerful presentation gives you a platform to communicate your message effectively, influence your audience and spark desired action. Effective presenters spend a considerable amount of time preparing for their presentation, ensuring that the structure, content and communication style is appropriate for their audience. It is often what happens before the presenter enters the room that dictates the success of the presentation.

Persuasive Presentation Skills includes the **Persuasive Presentation Skills Presentation Planner**, provided as a free downloadable tool.

Learning Objectives
- Explain the importance of preparation in delivering a successful presentation.
- Explain how to structure your presentation to deliver key messages.
- Describe how to connect with your audience and maintain attention.
- Identify key factors for enhancing your message and projecting credibility.
- How to design and use visual aids to support your message.
- Describe how to control your nervous energy.
- Create a Skill Development Action Plan.

Course Content
- Part 1: Preparation Fundamentals
- Part 2: Presentation Structure
- Part 3: Connecting with Your Audience
- Part 4: Developing an Individual Presentation Style
- Part 5: Tips and Tricks for Getting Your Message Across
- Part 6: Creating Effective Support Materials
- Part 7: Mastering Nervous Energy

Making Meetings Work
Getting the Most out of Meetings

Course Content

- Part 1: Types of Meetings
- Part 2: Why Meetings Fail
- Part 3: Solutions to Meeting Barriers
- Part 4: Planning the Meeting
- Part 5: Preparing the Agenda
- Part 6: Conducting the Meeting

Learning Short-take® Outline

Making Meetings Work combines self-study with realistic workplace activities to provide you with the key skills and techniques to make meetings work. Your meetings will become more focused, efficient, targeted and more likely to have a productive impact on the company's bottom-line. You will learn how to more effectively prepare, manage, facilitate and actively participate in meetings.

It is estimated that the average professional spends 61.5 hours per month in meetings, or two weeks every year. It is also estimated that at least 50% of this time is wasted in unproductive meeting activity. **Making Meetings Work** will provide you with the tools to help you save time and money.

Making Meetings Work includes the **Meeting Administration Checklist, Meeting Agenda** and **Meeting Minutes** provided as free downloadable tools.

Learning Objectives

- Evaluate your current level of meeting success.
- Identify the various types of meetings and explain key differences.
- Develop solutions to common meeting problems.
- Outline the steps for a successful meeting.
- Carry out meeting planning and preparation.
- Create a Skill Development Action Plan.

Confident Facilitation Skills
Tools and Techniques for the Professional Facilitator

Learning Short-take® Outline

Confident Facilitation Skills combines self-study with realistic workplace activities to provide you with the key skills and techniques to become a more effective facilitator. You will be guided through a comprehensive approach to prepare for a facilitation session, focus the group, draw out ideas, manage difficult behavior, build consensus, maintain high energy, close the session, and construct customized agendas. **Confident Facilitation Skills** also includes a comprehensive reference guide of proven group facilitation techniques.

Facilitation is fast becoming a key skill for anyone who is in a team, leading a project team, heading up a working group, or managing a department. Facilitation is the skill and art of guiding others to solve problems to achieve objectives without personally giving advice or offering solutions. A facilitator provides the structure and process - enabling groups to function effectively and make high-quality decisions.

Confident Facilitation Skills includes the **Confident Facilitation Initial Meeting Tool**, provided to you as a free download.

Learning Objectives
- Define the role of a facilitator.
- Identify the key facilitation principles.
- Describe best practices related to each facilitation principle.
- Differentiate between process and content facilitation.
- Identify the core practices and skills required for effective facilitation.
- Explain how to stimulate group participation and positively handle conflict.
- Create a Skill Development Action Plan.

Course Content
- Part 1: Facilitation Defined
- Part 2: The Role of the Facilitator
- Part 3: Key Principles of Facilitation
- Part 4: Content versus Process
- Part 5: Encouraging Group Participation
- Part 6: Managing Group Conflict

www.catherinemattiske.com